# Progressive

# ROCK GUITAR METHOD

by
**Brett Duncan**

---

**Visit our Website**
# www.learntoplaymusic.com

*The Progressive Series of Music Instruction Books, CDs, and DVDs*

## CD TRACK LISTING

1  Tuning Notes

2  Lesson 2 Ex 1,2

3  Lesson 3 Ex 3-5

4  Lesson 4 Ex 6,7

5  Lesson 5 Ex 8

6  Lesson 6 Ex 9 -
   Going Uptown - Lead

7  Lesson 7 Ex 10-15

8  Lesson 8 Ex 16-17

9  Lesson 9 - On the Seventh Day

10  Lesson 10 - Rockin' the Country

11  Lesson 11 Ex 18-23

12  Lesson 12 Ex 24 -
    Three O'clock Blues - Lead

13  Lesson 13 Ex 26
    Seven Miles From Memphis - Lead

14  Lesson 14 Ex 27-29

15  Lesson 15 Ex 30-
    Ballad for the Major - Rhythm

16  Lesson 16 Ex 31-33

17  Lesson 17 Ex 34 - Sixteen Years - Lead

18  Lesson 18 Ex 36-38

19  Lesson 19 Ex 39-41

20  Lesson 20 Ex 42-46

**PROGRESSIVE ROCK GUITAR METHOD**
**I.S.B.N. 0 947183 92 2**
**Order Code: CP-18392**

**Acknowledgments**
Cover Photograph: Phil Martin
Photographs: Phil Martin

For more information on this series contact;
L.T.P. Publishing Pty Ltd
email: info@learntoplaymusic.com
or visit our website;
**www.learntoplaymusic.com**

# Contents

# Introduction

*Progressive Rock Guitar Method* will introduce you to the exciting world of Rock guitar. It will not be necessary to have any previous knowledge of the guitar, as this book is suitable for the complete beginner. Experienced guitarists however, who perhaps have not tackled this style before, will find this manual invaluable as an introduction to the basics of Rock guitar.

This book deals with the two main classifications of Rock guitar, rhythm and lead. You will become familiar with both subjects as you work your way through the book.

Rhythm guitar, being the technique of strumming chords, is explained clearly and simply throughout the book, with the help of an easy read system involving arrows. Lead guitar, being the picking of individual notes, is explained with the use of tablature, an easy read system for reading notes. Throughout the book there are many songs which use the various techniques detailed in each lesson. You will be invited to try both the rhythm and lead part to each song.

A special section dealing with tuning, the basics of music for Rock guitar and a chord chart has been included at the end of the book.

It is recommended that you should have a copy of the accompanying recording that includes all the examples in this book. The book shows you where to place your fingers and what technique to use and the tape lets you hear how each example should sound.

Once you have successfully completed this book you will be able to further your study of Rock guitar by immediately moving onto *Progressive Rock Guitar Technique* which deals with the more advanced aspects of Rock Guitar.

Good luck and have fun,
Brett Duncan

# SECTION 1

# Basic Rock Progressions, Basic Rock Riffs

# Lesson 1
## Getting Started

Lesson One will introduce you to several important basic points before you begin Rock guitar. They are the parts of the guitar, holding the guitar, right and left hand technique.

## The Parts of the Guitar

It will be helpful to know the parts of the acoustic and electric guitars as shown below.

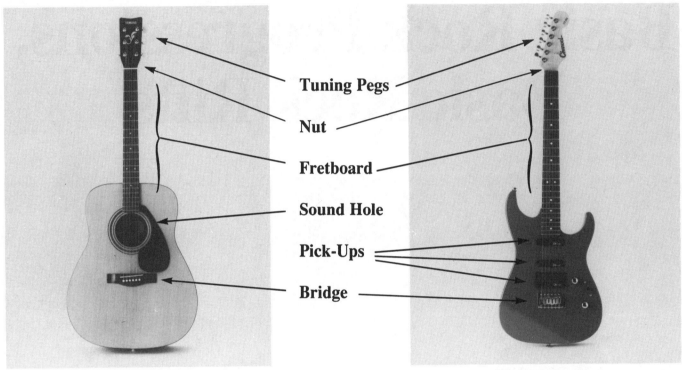

Tuning Pegs

Nut

Fretboard

Sound Hole

Pick-Ups

Bridge

*Acoustic guitar*

*Electric guitar*

## Holding the Guitar

Although most Rock guitarists perform standing up, it is recommended to practice the examples and songs in this book in a seated position. The chair must be of a comfortable height and the right leg should be raised with the help of a footstool. You may also find a music stand a useful aid in your practice.

*Practice position*

# Right Hand Technique

The traditional picking grip is holding the pick with the thumb and the last joint of the first finger. There are variations on this grip but I recommend trying this method as it will prove more efficient in most applications.

There are basically two right hand positions when using the pick. The first is closing the fingers of the right hand, and the second position is opening the hand across the face of the guitar. Try both positions and decide which you are comfortable with.

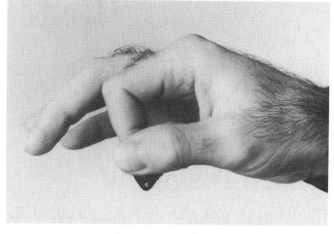

*Hold pick with thumb and first finger*

*Position 1*

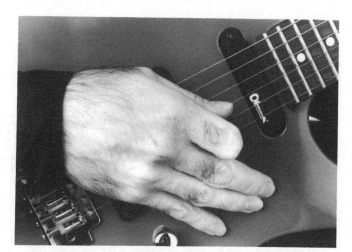

*Position 2*

# Left Hand Technique

All notes must be fretted with the tips of the fingers and positioned as close as practical to the fretwires. The left hand thumb must be positioned behind the neck of the guitar.

*Fingertips as close as practical to fretwires*

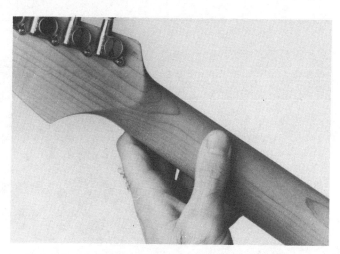

*Positioned thumb at the back of the neck*

# Lesson 2
## Basic Chords

The first chords to learn when playing Rock Guitar are the basic chords found within the first four frets of the guitar. These are the easiest chords to play on the guitar and will be used for all the Rock chord progressions throughout this book.

## Chord Diagrams

Chords are learnt with the help of a chord diagram. This will show you exactly where you must put your left fingers in order to play a particular chord. A chord diagram is a grid of horizontal and vertical lines representing the strings and frets of the guitar as shown below. The example given is the A Major chord.

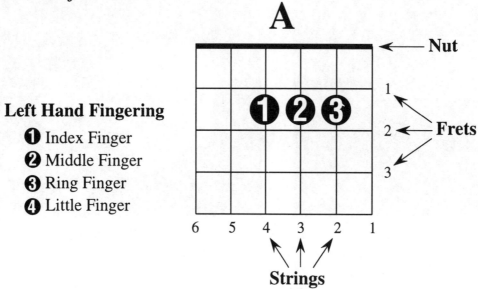

**Left Hand Fingering**

❶ Index Finger
❷ Middle Finger
❸ Ring Finger
❹ Little Finger

If you read the above chord diagram correctly then you should find that your first finger of your left hand is on the fourth string; second fret, your second finger is on the third string; second fret, and your third finger is on the second string; second fret as shown in the photo below.

*A Major Chord*

# Strumming

The first type of strum used in this book is the down-strum. The right hand strikes across the strings in a downward motion from the sixth string to the first string.

A down-strum will be indicated by a downward pointing arrow as shown below. For the first example, an A Major chord is fingered with the left hand as the right hand strums four down-strums.

## Example 1

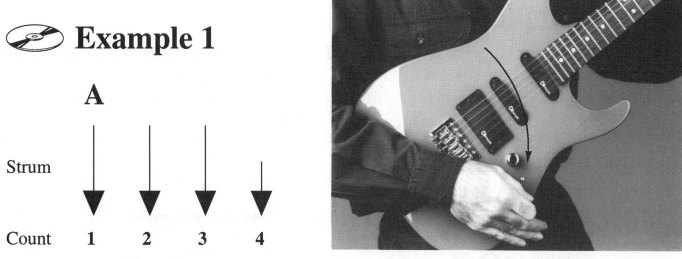

*The Down Strum*

# Chord Progressions

**Staff:** A standard music staff will be used to show you which chords have to be played and how long a certain chord must be played for. The music staff consists of five lines with a treble clef at the beginning of the staff.

**Bars:** The staff is divided into sections called bars or measures. The bars are separated by a vertical line called a bar line with a double bar line to mark the end of a progression. There are four "beats" or four "counts" to every bar as indicated by the time signature at the beginning of the staff. At this stage you will strum one down-strum on every beat of the bar. Example Two shows an A Major chord being strummed for four bars.

## Example 2

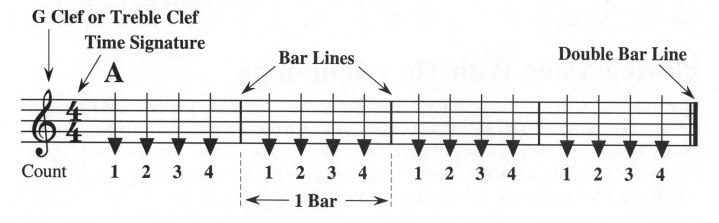

# Lesson 3
## Basic Rock Progressions

The examples in this lesson will introduce you to your first basic chords and how these chords can be used in a basic Rock progression.

 ## Example 3

Example Three features the chords A Major and D Major. The A Major chord is played for the first two bars of the progression before changing to the D Major chord for bars three and four. Remember, there are four beats to every bar and you will strum one down-strum to every beat.

Study the following chord diagrams carefully and double check that you are holding down the right string on the correct fret.

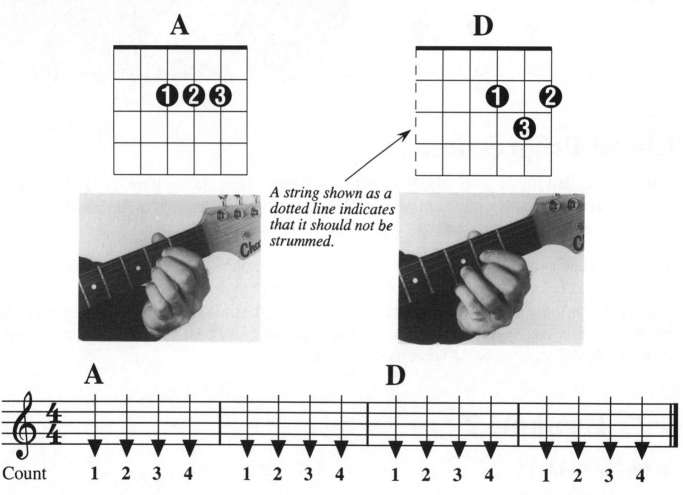

A string shown as a dotted line indicates that it should not be strummed.

## Playing Along With The CD or Tape

Listen to the accompanying recording to hear exactly how the above example should sound. Practice this example slowly at first, slowly increasing tempo. Once you are confident you can change from the A Major to the D Major, strumming evenly without stopping the beat, try playing along with the recording. You will hear a drum beat at the beginning of each example, to lead you into the example and to help you keep time.

# Example 4

The next example introduces the E Major chord. The diagram below shows the correct fingering for the E Major chord.

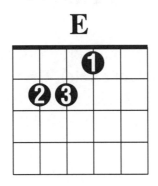

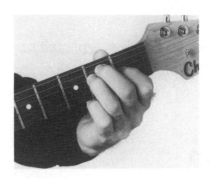

For Example Four an A Major chord is played for the first bar, a D Major is played for the second bar, and E Major is played for the third bar and the A Major is played again for the final bar.

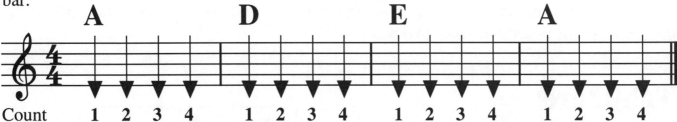

# Example 5

Example Five features a twelve bar Blues progression. This is a popular chord progression used in Blues and Rock and will appear frequently throughout the book. In order to play a twelve bar Blues progression using the chords you have learnt so far, play the chords in the sequence shown below.

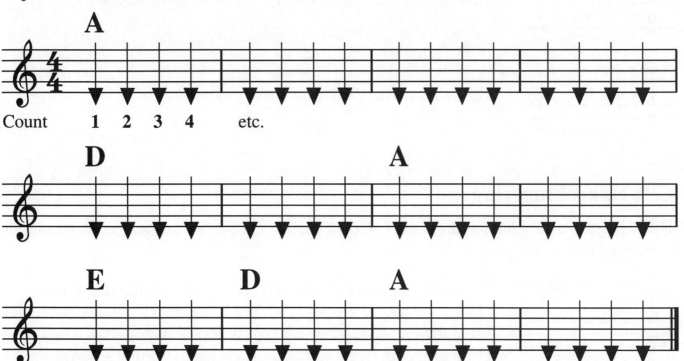

# Lesson 4
## Basic Rock Riffs

A "riff" is a pattern of notes repeated several times throughout a progression. The first riffs you will learn will be played within the first position (the first four frets). The riffs are progressively set out in order of difficulty and will accompany a basic Rock Progression.

## Notation

In order to play the riffs, licks and solos throughout this book a basic knowledge of notation is needed. This book uses standard music notation and tablature notation. If you cannot read music notes use the tab written below the music. Music readers will need to look at the tab to see what technique is being used to play certain notes (e.g. hammer, slide etc) and also which position on the fretboard the notes have to be played.

## Tablature

Tablature is a method of indicating the position of notes on the fretboard. There are six "tab" lines each representing one of the six strings on the guitar.

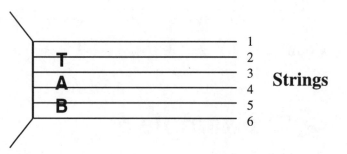

When a number is placed on one of the lines, it indicates the fret location of the note. e.g.

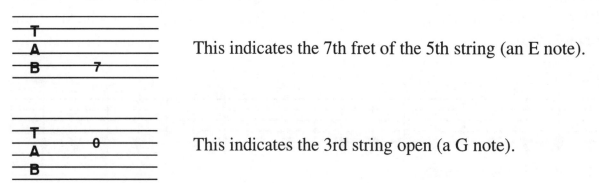

This indicates the 7th fret of the 5th string (an E note).

This indicates the 3rd string open (a G note).

## Left Hand Fingering

The suggested left hand fingering is shown below the tab. The fingers are numbered the same as mentioned earlier in Lesson 2.

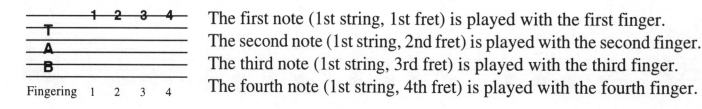

The first note (1st string, 1st fret) is played with the first finger.
The second note (1st string, 2nd fret) is played with the second finger.
The third note (1st string, 3rd fret) is played with the third finger.
The fourth note (1st string, 4th fret) is played with the fourth finger.

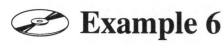 # Example 6

Below is an example of a basic rock riff and how it will be represented in tablature form. The tablature shows that the open 5th string is played four times for the duration of the 1st bar, the 2nd fret of the 5th is played for the 2nd bar, the 3rd fret of the 5th string is played for the 3rd bar and the open string is used once more for the final bar.

## Pick Motion: Down-Stroke

All notes in this riff are played with a downward motion of the right hand. This is indicated by the symbol **V** shown above the tablature. Attention should also be given to the suggested fingering shown below the tablature.

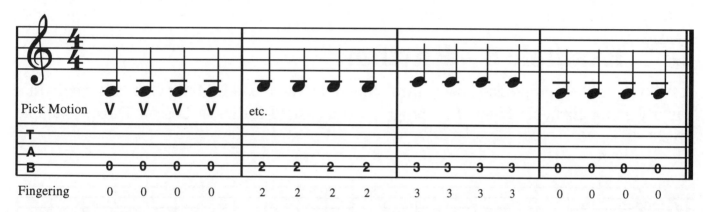

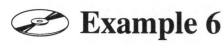 # Example 7

This time the riff will be played on the 4th, 5th and 6th strings. The first two bars of the riff are played on the 5th string, the next two bars are played on the 4th string, bars five and six are played on the 6th string and the final two bars are played on the fifth string.

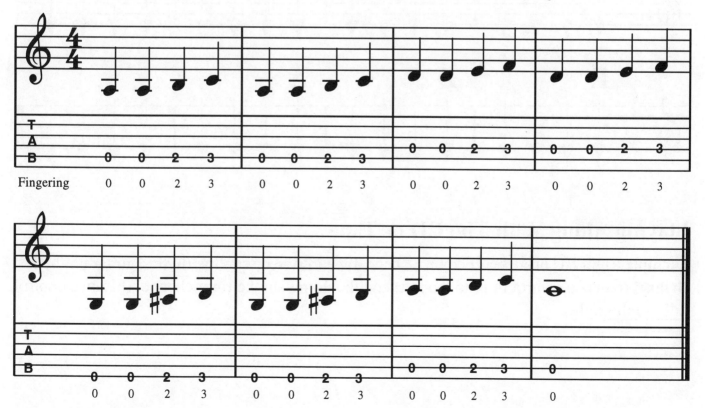

# Lesson 5
## Rhythm and Lead Guitar

Rock Guitar can be broken down into two different classifications, Rhythm guitar and Lead guitar. You will become familiar with both styles as you work your way through this book.

In this lesson you will learn how a chord progression and a riff can be played together as an accompaniment to each other. Rhythm guitar is the strumming and changing of chords through a chord progression (as discussed in Lesson Three), and Lead guitar is the picking of notes or riffs (Lesson Four).

 ## Example 8 – Rhythm

A twelve bar blues progression using the A Major, D Major and E Major chords is the rhythm guitar part for Example Eight. This progression appeared earlier in Lesson Three, Example Five.

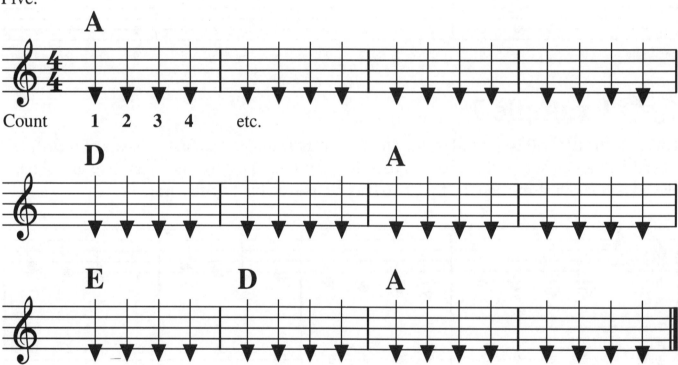

### Playing Along With The CD or Tape

Example Eight has been recorded on CD and Tape in stereo with the rhythm guitar on the left channel (balance control fully to the left) and the drums on the right channel (balance control fully to the right).

#  Example 8 – Lead

The riff or Lead guitar part to Example Eight is played on the three bass strings. As with previous riffs all notes are played with a down-stroke. The chord symbols for the accompanying rhythm guitar are indicated above the music staff.

On the recording the riff has been recorded on the right channel (balance control fully to the right) and the drums have been recorded on the left channel (balance control fully to the left).

#  Example 8 – Rhythm and Lead

Now that you have practiced both the rhythm guitar part (chord strumming), and the lead guitar part (riff), listen to the recording to hear both parts being played together. The rhythm guitar has been recorded on the left channel and the lead guitar has been recorded on the right channel.

# Lesson 6
## The Up-Strum

In this lesson you will learn how to use the up-strum. This means that the strings are strummed with an upward motion from the first string towards the sixth string. The up-strum is played exactly halfway between the down-strums. The word "and" is used to count an up-strum.

The following example shows the A chord being strummed down-up, down-up, down-up, down-up. The rhythm is counted 1 and 2 and 3 and 4 and.

## Example 9

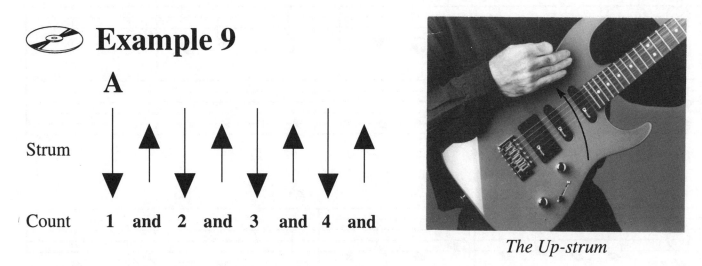

*The Up-strum*

## Going Uptown – Rhythm

Going Uptown is based upon a twelve bar blues progression and uses the rhythm shown above. The symbol **&** is used as an abbreviation for the up-strum count "and".

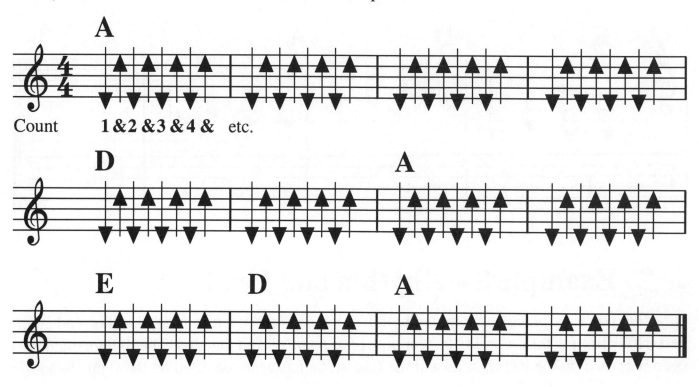

Count    **1 & 2 & 3 & 4 &**   etc.

# Going Uptown – Lead

As with the previous examples the riff or lead guitar part to Going Uptown is mainly played on the bass strings.

## Pick Motion: Up-Stroke

An up-stroke of the pick is also introduced in Going Uptown. This means that a note must be played with an upward motion of the pick. The symbol **Λ** will indicate when a note must be played with an up-stroke.

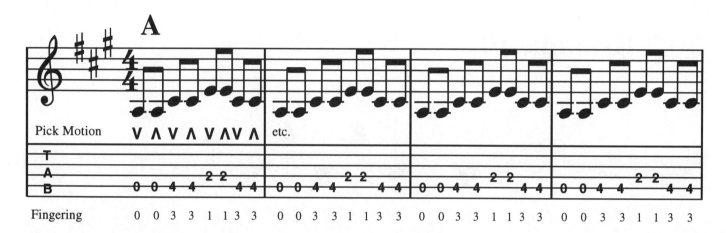

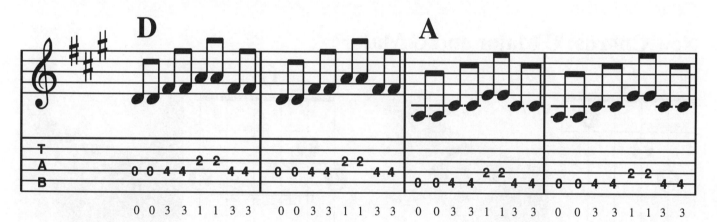

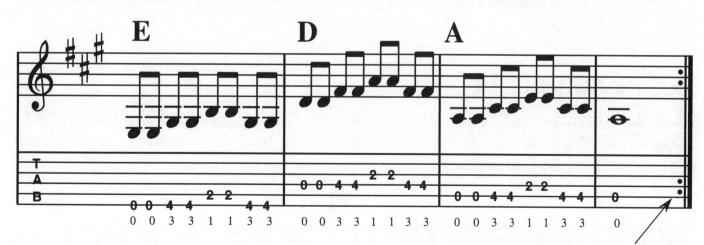

**Repeat Sign:** A thick line, a thin line and two dots indicates a repeat sign. Repeat the example from the beginning.

# Lesson 7
## Rhythm Patterns

Different rhythm patterns can be created by eliminating some of the up-strokes within a bar. For example, in the rhythm pattern shown below the up-strum which immediately follows the first beat is not played. This creates a rhythm of 1, 2 and 3 and 4 and. Listen to this example on the recording to help with the correct timing of this rhythm. Once again an A Major chord is used.

 ## Example 10

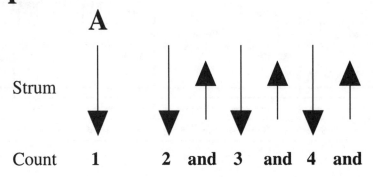

## New Chords: C Major and G Major

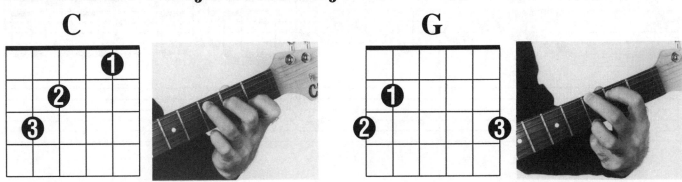

 ## Example 11

Apply the rhythm used in Example 10 to the following chord progression which features the C Major and G Major chords. After repeating the first four bars, the progression is completed with one strum of the C Major chord.

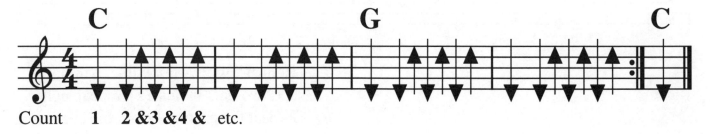

## ⊙ Example 12

This time the up-strums following the first and third beats are eliminated to create the rhythm 1, 2 and 3, 4 and. The C Major chord is used.

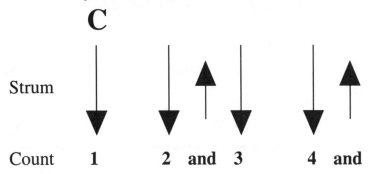

## ⊙ Example 13

Now apply the rhythm shown in Example 12 to the following chord progression.

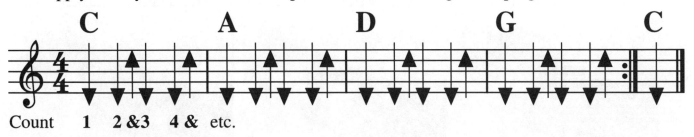

## ⊙ Example 14

The final rhythm in this lesson is counted 1 and 2 and 3, 4. The C Major chord is used.

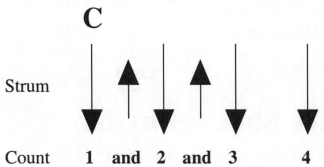

## ⊙ Example 15

Now try the rhythm used in Example 14 with the following chord progression. This time there are two chords to each bar with each chord having the value of two beats.

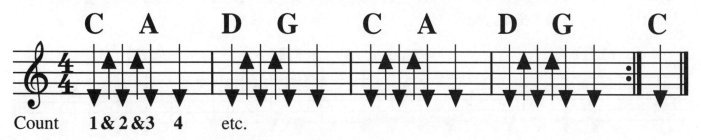

# Lesson 8
# Minor Chords

The next type of chord you will learn is the Minor chord. Minor chords have a more "haunting" or "creepy" sound than Major chords. The most common basic Minor chords are the A Minor, D Minor and E Minor chords.

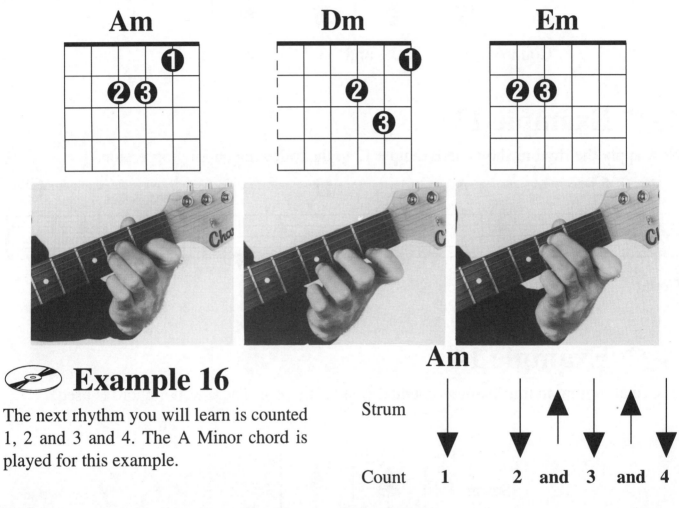

**Am**     **Dm**     **Em**

 ## Example 16

The next rhythm you will learn is counted 1, 2 and 3 and 4. The A Minor chord is played for this example.

**Am**

| Strum | | | | | | |
| Count | 1 | | 2 | and | 3 | and | 4 |

 ## Coal Miner Blues – Rhythm

The A Minor, D Minor and E Minor chords are used for Coal Miner Blues. The rhythm is as in Example 16.

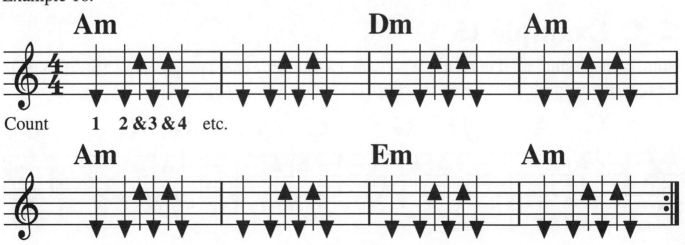

**Am**          **Dm**     **Am**

Count    1    2 & 3 & 4    etc.

**Am**          **Em**     **Am**

# Coal Miner Blues – Lead

Now try the lead guitar part to Coal Miner Blues.

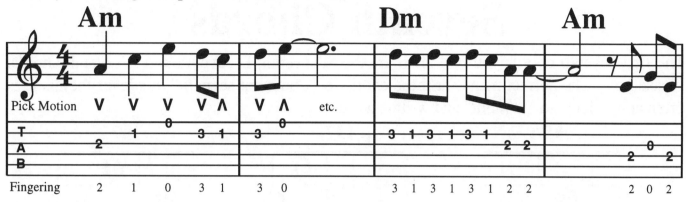

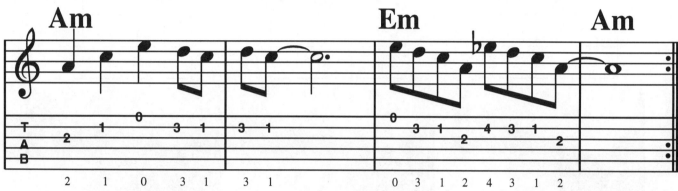

## New Chord: B Minor

The sixth and fifth strings should be avoided when strumming B Minor.

## Two Bar Rhythms

Until now the same rhythm has been used throughout a chord progression. It is possible

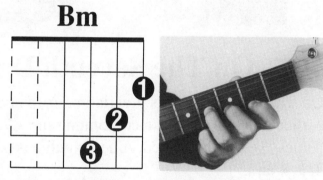

however to change the rhythm during a progression. The rhythm used for the following example alternates between two different rhythm patterns. The rhythm used for the first bar is 1, 2, 3 and 4 and. The rhythm used for the second bar is 1 and 2 and 3, 4. The rhythm used for the third bar is the same as the first bar, the fourth bar is the same as the second bar and so on.

# Example 17

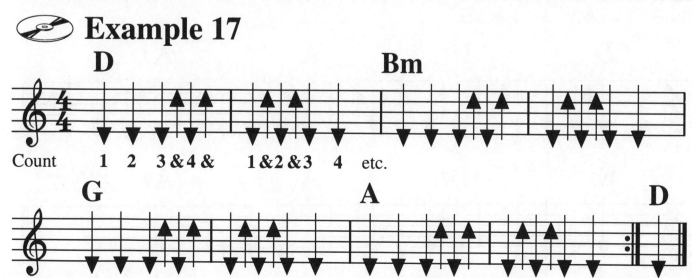

# Lesson 9
## Seventh Chords

The first seventh chords you will learn are the A seventh, D seventh and E seventh chords. Please note: The correct name for these chords is "dominant seventh", however the name is often abbreviated to "seventh" and written as such.

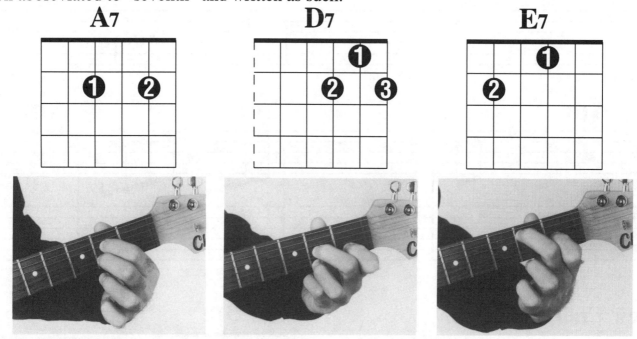

A7       D7       E7

## On The Seventh Day – Rhythm

On The Seventh Day is a variation of the twelve bar Blues progression which has appeared earlier in the book. By incorporating the A7, D7 and E7 chords into the progression, a more "bluesy" effect is created. A new rhythm is used for the example. The rhythm is counted 1 and 2, 3, 4 and.

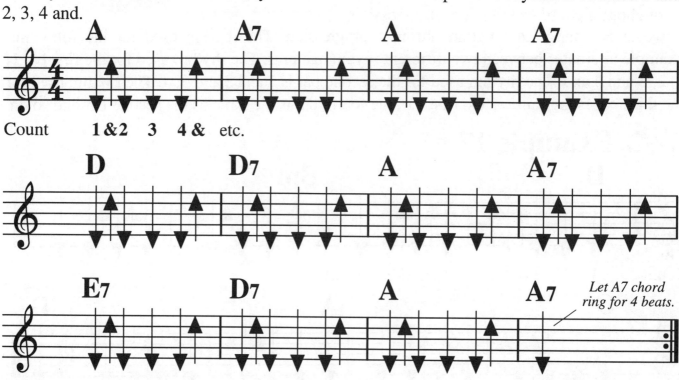

Let A7 chord ring for 4 beats.

# ⊙ On The Seventh Day – Lead

This time every string is used to play the lead guitar riff which accompanies the rhythm to On The Seventh Day. Special attention should be given to the suggested pick motion of the right hand and the left hand fingering.

## Alternative Fingerings

The A seventh and E seventh are two chords which have an alternative fingering. These fingerings are more difficult but will tend to be used in most situations. Use these fingerings once you become confident with chords.

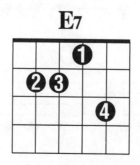

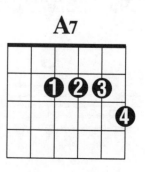

# Lesson 10
## More Seventh Chords

This lesson features two new seventh chords, the G7 and C7. The diagrams below show the correct fingering for both chords.

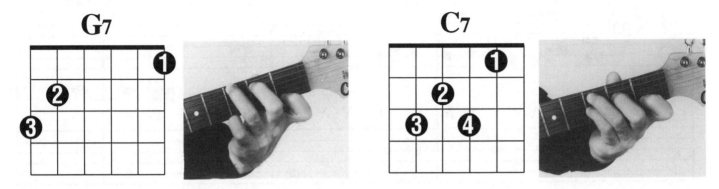

The G seventh and C seventh chords will appear in the following song. This time a longer chord progression is used. Rockin' The Country is sixteen bars long and has a country-rock sound to it. The rhythm chosen for this example is 1, 2 and 3, 4 and.

## 🖸 Rockin' The Country – Rhythm

# Rockin' The Country – Lead

Now try the lead guitar part to Rockin' The Country.

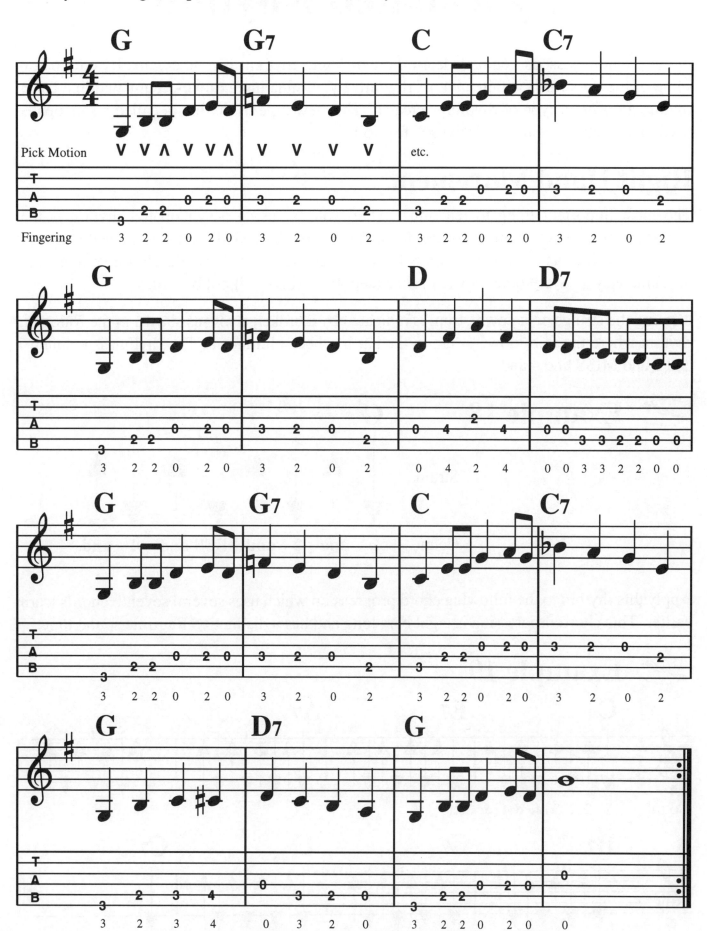

# Lesson 11
## Syncopated Rhythm

In the previous lessons you have learnt how different rhythms can be created by eliminating some of the up-strums within a bar of rhythm. By eliminating a **down-strum** within a bar of rhythm a different type of rhythm is created. This new type of rhythm is called a syncopated rhythm and has a distinctive "calypso" feel to it.

## Right Hand Movement

The most important thing to remember when you are using a syncopated rhythm is that although you will not strum one of the down strums, the right hand must still move downwards across the strings as if a down-strum is being played. The right hand should move in exactly the same way as every other down-strum except the strings will not be struck.

Missing the strings on a down-strum is indicated by a broken arrow as shown in the following rhythm where the third down-strum in the bar has been eliminated. The rhythm is counted 1 and 2 and MISS and 4 and.

## Example 18

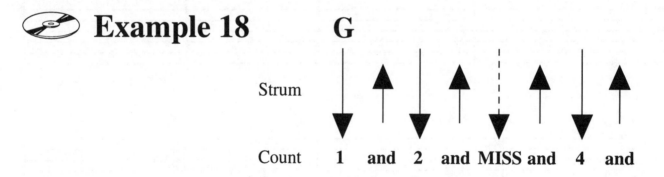

Apply this rhythm to the following chord progression which uses several seventh chords learnt earlier. This chord progression is eight bars long and has a distinctive Ragtime sound to it.

## Example 19

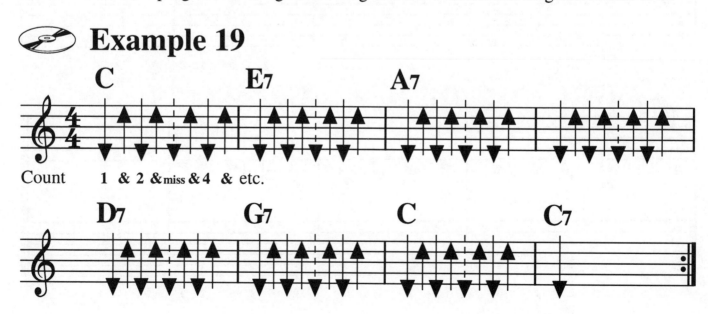

# Example 20

Now try some variations using syncopated rhythm. The first variation is the same rhythm used in the previous two examples except the up-strum between the first and second beat has been eliminated. The rhythm is counted, 1, 2 and MISS and 4 and.

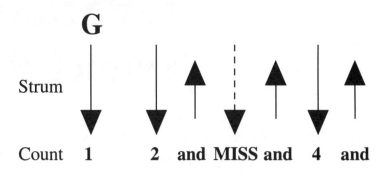

## New Chord: F Major

The F Major chord is one of the most difficult basic chords to learn. This is mainly because the first finger of the left hand must fret the first and second strings at the same time (as indicated by the curved line). When a finger frets two or more notes across a fret at the same time it is called a bar.

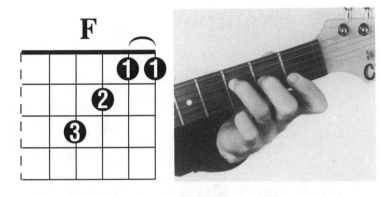

 # Example 21

Example 21 uses the rhythm learnt in Example 20. The new chord, F Major is also used.

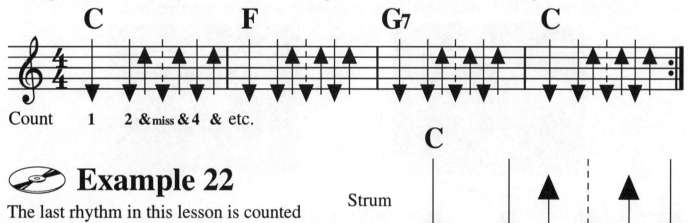

# Example 22

The last rhythm in this lesson is counted 1, 2 and MISS and 4.

# Example 23

Apply this rhythm to the following chord progression.

# Lesson 12
## Triplet Rhythm

One of the most popular rhythms used in Rock guitar is the triplet rhythm. This means that three strums are played to every beat. A new word is used to help count triplet rhythm – "ah". To count a triplet rhythm say 1 and ah, 2 and ah, 3 and ah, 4 and ah. In order to get the right sound for the triplet rhythm, the first strum of each group of three strums is played louder. Example 24 shows the A7 chord being strummed for one bar using a triplet rhythm. The symbol > is used to show which strums are to be played louder.

### Example 24  A7

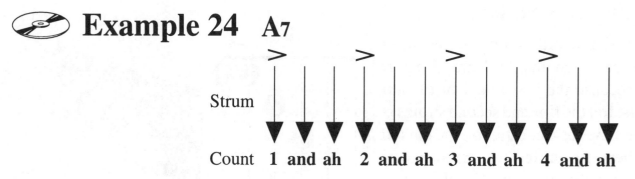

## Long and Short Strums

Using long and short strums is a handy way of getting used to a triplet rhythm. A long strum is a normal down-strum, striking across all or most of the strings. Using a short strum only requires the right hand to strum the middle two or three strings of the guitar. The photos below show approximately which strings are strummed using long and short strums.

*Long Strum*

*Short Strum*

Applying this principal to a triplet rhythm will help achieve the correct "feel" for triplet rhythm. A long strum is used on every beat and a short strum is used on the "ands" and "ahs". Long and short strums are illustrated by the use of a long arrow and a short arrow as shown below.

### Example 25  A7

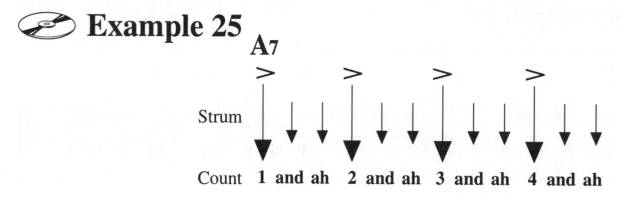

## New Chord: B Seventh

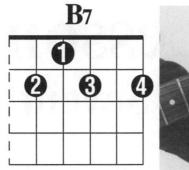

 # Three O'Clock Blues – Rhythm

Three O'Clock Blues is an eight bar blues progression with a distinctive "blues" sound. The triplet rhythm shown in Example 25 is played throughout the progression. The symbol ⁒ means repeat the previous rhythm patterns. The new chord B7 will also be used.

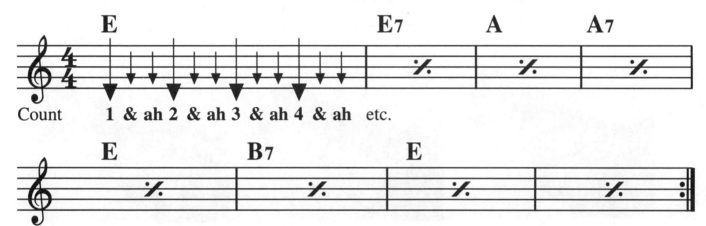

Count   1 & ah 2 & ah 3 & ah 4 & ah  etc.

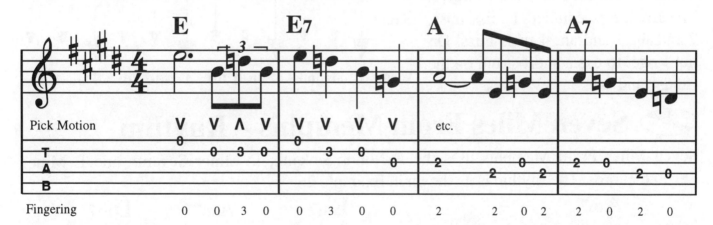

# Three O'Clock Blues – Lead

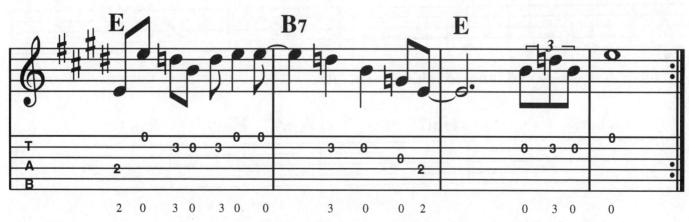

# Lesson 13
## Minor Seventh Chords

The next type of chord you will learn is the Minor Seventh chord. The most common basic Minor Seventh chords are the A Minor Seventh, D Minor Seventh and E Minor Seventh chords.

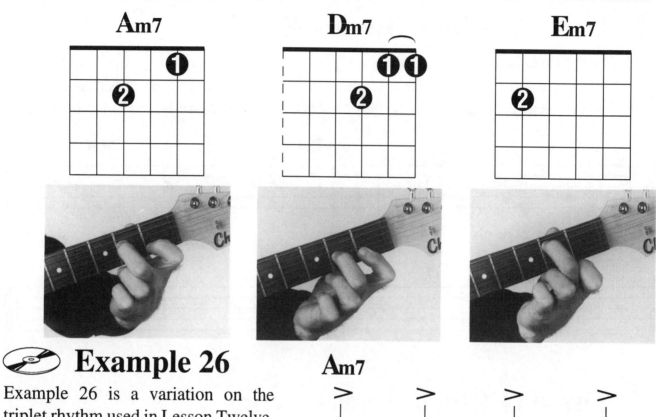

Am7          Dm7          Em7

### Example 26

Example 26 is a variation on the triplet rhythm used in Lesson Twelve. The rhythm is counted 1 miss miss, 2 and ah, 3 and ah, 4 miss miss. Do not forget to use a short strum on the "ands" and "ahs".

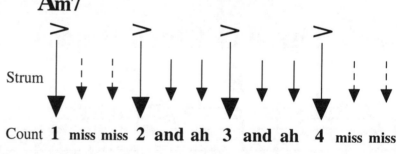

Am7

Strum

Count **1** miss miss **2 and ah 3 and ah 4** miss miss

### Seven Miles From Memphis – Rhythm

Seven Miles From Memphis uses the A Minor Seventh, D Minor Seventh and E Minor Seventh chords. The rhythm is as shown in Example 26.

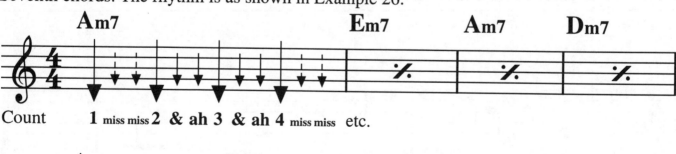

Am7          Em7     Am7     Dm7

Count     **1** miss miss **2 & ah 3 & ah 4** miss miss  etc.

Am7          Dm7     Am7  Em7  Am7

# Seven Miles From Memphis – Lead

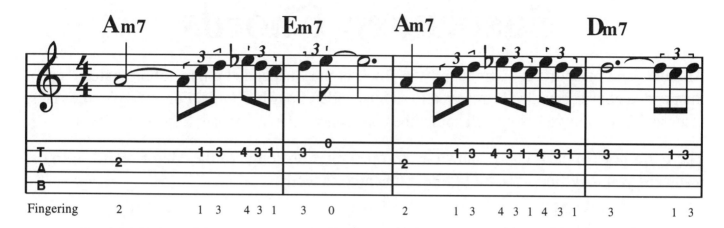

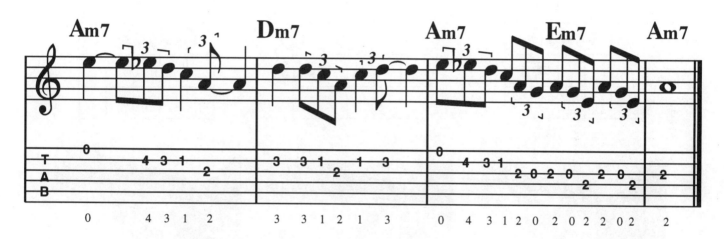

# Lesson 14
## Suspended Chords

Another type of chord used frequently in Rock is the Suspended chord (abbreviated "sus"). Suspended chords can also be referred to as Suspended Fourth Chords. For example, the Asus, Dsus and Esus shown below will sometimes be seen written as Asus4, Dsus4 and Esus4.

The extra note in each chord shown as an open circle belongs to the Major chord. In most instances you may find it useful to finger this note as well.

### Asus    Dsus    Esus

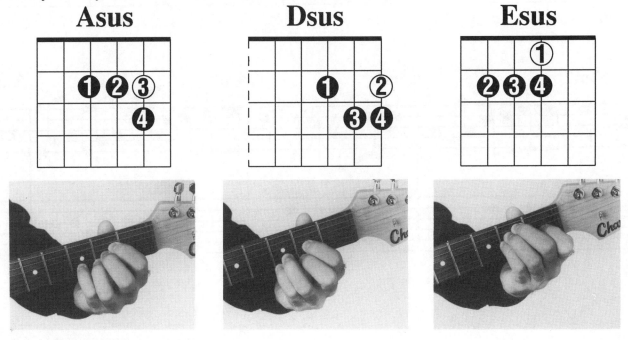

### Example 27

The following chord progression uses the above suspended chords with a two bar rhythm. The symbol 𝄍 placed between two bars will indicate an exact repeat of the previous two bars.

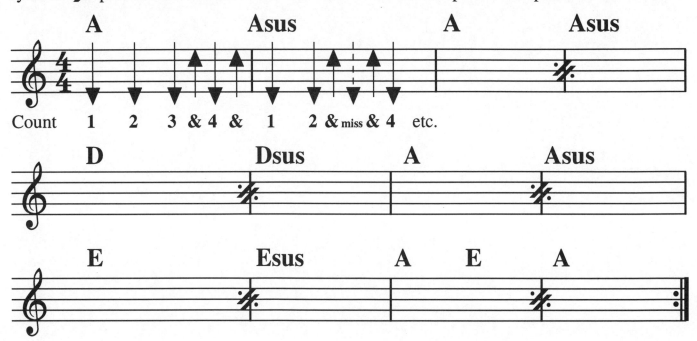

# Changing Chords on Up-Strums

Until now every time you have changed to a new chord it has been on a down-strum. One of the most difficult techniques of basic strumming is changing to a new chord on an up-strum. In Example 28, begin by strumming an A Major chord but change to the A Suspended chord on the up-strum between beats 2 and 3.

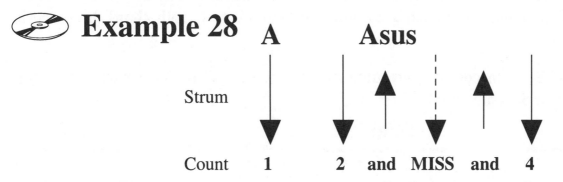

Apply this principal to the chord progression below using three new chords – the C Suspended, F Suspended and G Suspended chords.

## New chords: Csus, Fsus, Gsus

*The cross here indicates that the fifth string must be muted. This is achieved by gently touching the string with the third finger.*

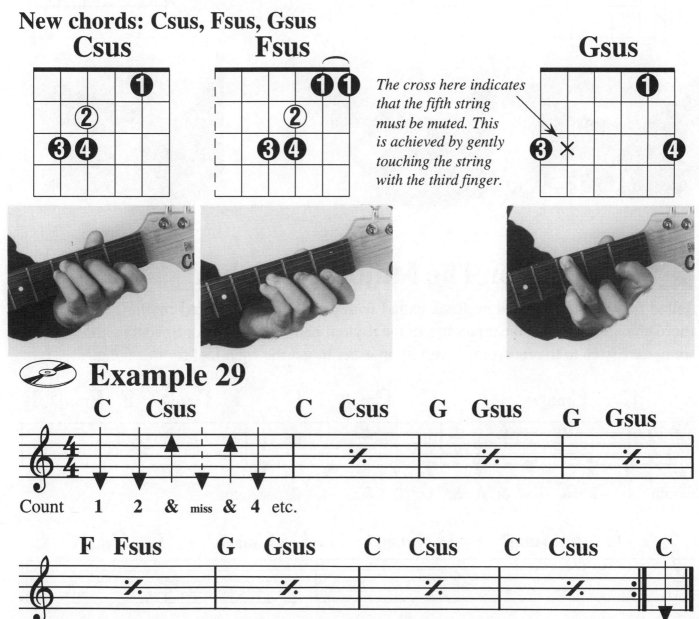

# Lesson 15
## Major Seventh Chords

This lesson introduces the Major Seventh chord. The Major Seventh chord is a very pleasant sounding chord and should not be confused with the Dominant Seventh chord discussed in Lessons Nine and Ten.

Three basic Major Seventh chords used often in Rock are the C Major Seventh, F Major Seventh and G Major Seventh chords.

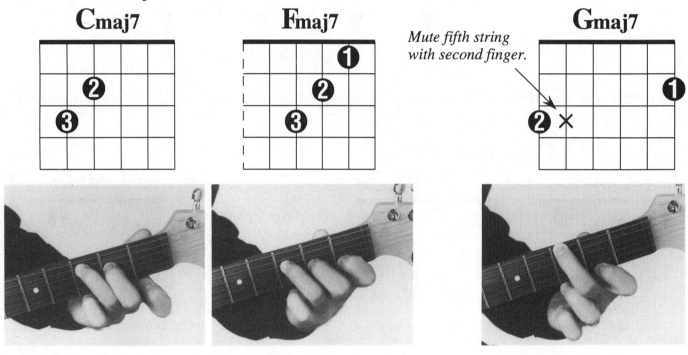

## Ballad For The Major – Rhythm

Ballad for the Major is a slow Rock ballad with a two bar syncopated rhythm. Many of the chord changes occur on the up-strums of the rhythm pattern. The Major Seventh chords shown are used. Listen to the recording carefully in order to get the right feel for this song.

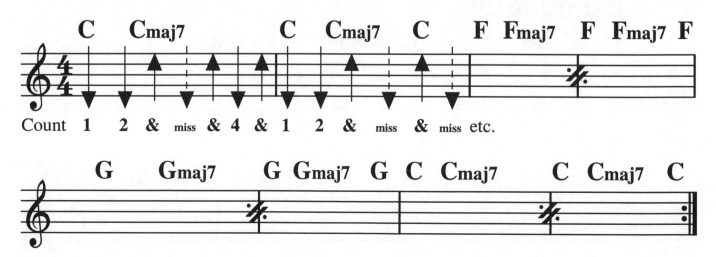

# Ballad For The Major – Lead

Fingering  1 0 2 0      1 3   0 3      1 0 3 1   2 2 2

3 0 0   2 0 2   3 0 0   2 0 2   4 3 1 3   0 2   1 3   1

## New Chords: Amaj7, Dmaj7

Two more popular Major Seventh chords are the A Major Seventh and D Major Seventh.

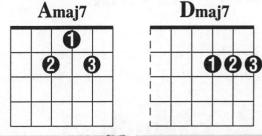

 # Example 30

Example 30 uses the A Major Seventh and D Major Seventh chords with almost every chord change occurring on an up-strum.

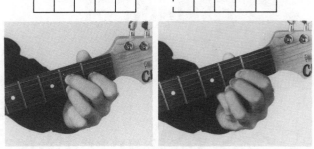

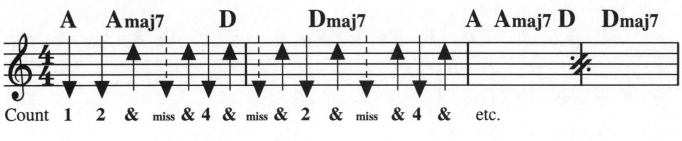

Count  **1** **2** & miss & **4** & miss & **2** & miss & **4** & etc.

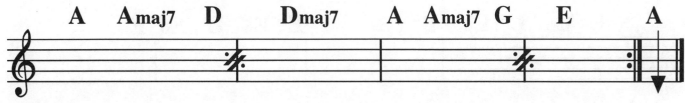

# Lesson 16
# Major Sixth Chords

Major sixth chords are another type of chord which can be used in Rock. These chords can be referred to as either "Major Sixth" or simply as "Sixth". For example, an A Major Sixth chord may be abbreviated to either "Amaj6" or "A6". Try the following Major Sixth chords.

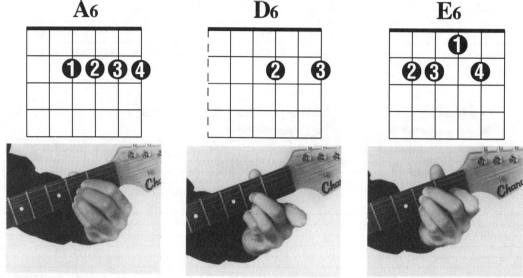

## Swing Rhythm

A swing rhythm is produced by slightly delaying the up-strum within a rhythm pattern, therefore giving the down-strum a longer time value than the up-strum. The rhythm to Example 31 is counted 1…ah, 2…ah, 3…ah, 4…ah. Listen to the recording to help get the feel for this rhythm.

## Example 31

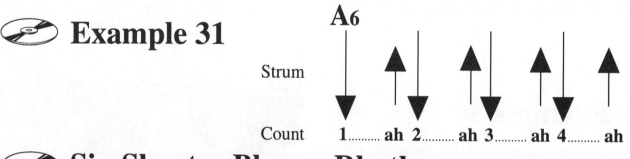

## Six-Shooter Blues – Rhythm

Six-Shooter Blues combines the swing rhythm with the E Major Sixth and A Major Sixth chords. Extra care is needed as a chord change occurs on almost every beat of the bar.

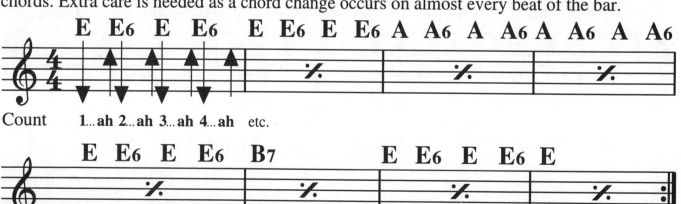

## Six-Shooter Blues – Lead

## Three Quarter Time

Until now all songs and examples have been in four quarter time (four beats to the bar). A $\frac{3}{4}$ time signature at the beginning of the music indicates that there are only three beats to every bar. The following example is counted 1, 2 and 3 and. As with $\frac{4}{4}$ time, the first beat of the bar should be played louder.

## Example 32

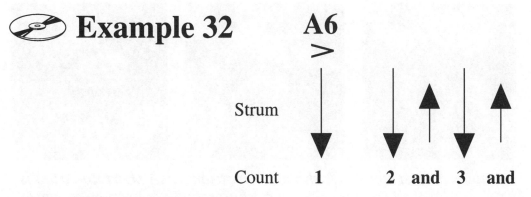

## Example 33

Apply the $\frac{3}{4}$ time rhythm in Example 32 to the following chord progression which uses the D Major Sixth, D Major Seventh and D Seventh chords.

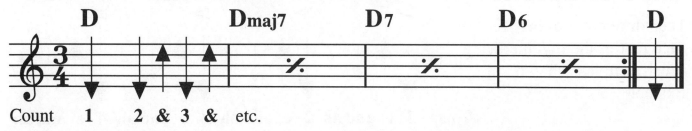

# Lesson 17
## Sixteenth Note Rhythm

Lesson 17 introduces the sixteenth note rhythm. A sixteenth note rhythm is created by strumming four strums to every beat, a total of sixteen strums to every bar. The syllable "e" is used in conjunction with the familiar syllables "and" and "ah" to count the sixteenth note rhythm. Example 34 is counted 1 e and ah, 2 e and ah, 3 e and ah, 4 e and ah, with each beat of the bar played louder. The C Major Seventh chord is used.

 **Example 34** Cmaj7

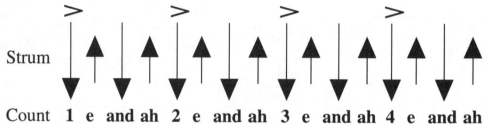

Strum

Count 1 e and ah 2 e and ah 3 e and ah 4 e and ah

### Right Hand Technique

In order to achieve the correct sound for the sixteenth note rhythm, it is important to strike the correct strings with the right hand. The following photos show approximately which strings are strummed on each part of the rhythm. On each beat of the bar a normal down-strum is used, a normal up-strum is used on the "e", a short down-strum is used for the "and", and a short up-strum for the "ah".

| **The Beat** | **"e"** | **"and"** | **"ah"** |
|:---:|:---:|:---:|:---:|
|  |  |  |  |
| *A normal down-strum is used on each beat of the bar.* | *A normal up-strum is used on the "e".* | *A short down-strum is used for "and".* | *A short up-strum is used for "ah".* |

 **Example 35**

Cmaj7

The different strums for each part of the rhythm are illustrated as shown in Example 35.

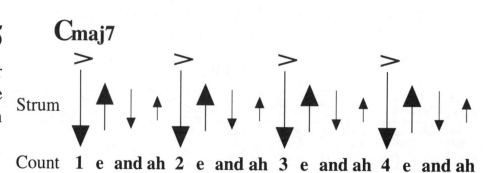

Strum

Count 1 e and ah 2 e and ah 3 e and ah 4 e and ah

## Sixteen Years – Rhythm

One application of the sixteenth note rhythm is its use in slow songs such as ballads etc. Most Rock songs which have a noticeably slow tempo will require a sixteenth note rhythm.

Sixteen Years is a slow Rock ballad which uses the sixteenth note rhythm shown in Example 35 and features many chords which have appeared in recent lessons.

## Sixteen Years – Lead

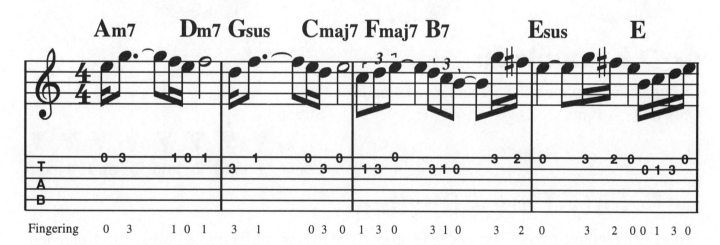

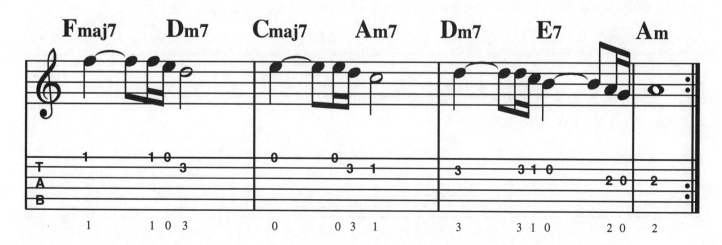

# Lesson 18
## Fifth Chords

Fifth chords (also known as "Rock chords" or "Power chords") consist of only two notes. Technically fifth chords are not actually chords because a chord requires three or more notes, but as they are used frequently in modern music it is becoming more and more acceptable to refer to these shapes as chords. The three popular fifth chords in the open position are the A5, D5 and E5. Remember only two strings are played with each chord.

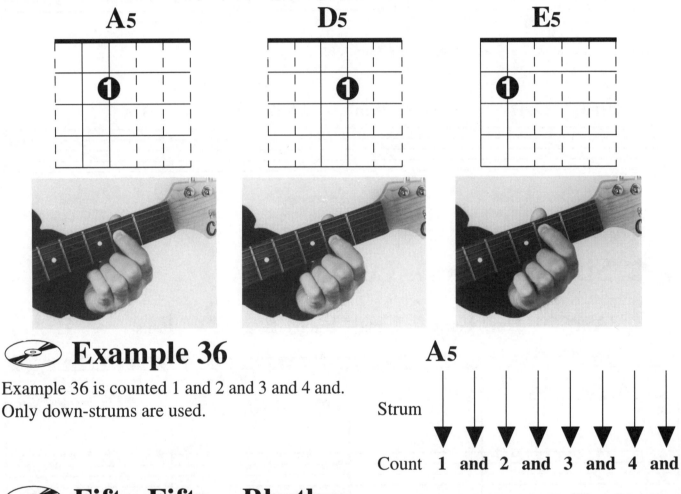

### 🎵 Example 36

Example 36 is counted 1 and 2 and 3 and 4 and. Only down-strums are used.

**A5**

Strum

Count  1  and  2  and  3  and  4  and

### 🎵 Fifty-Fifty – Rhythm

Fifty Fifty features the A5, D5 and E5 chords. The rhythm in Example 36 is used throughout and as only two strings are played, each strum is represented by a small arrow.

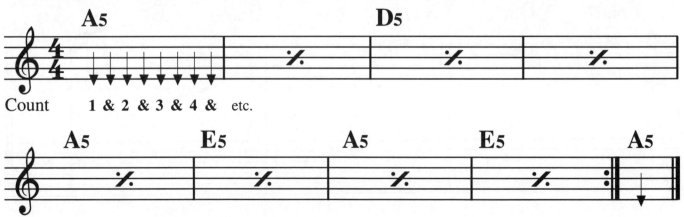

Count    1 & 2 & 3 & 4 &   etc.

## Fifty Fifty – Lead

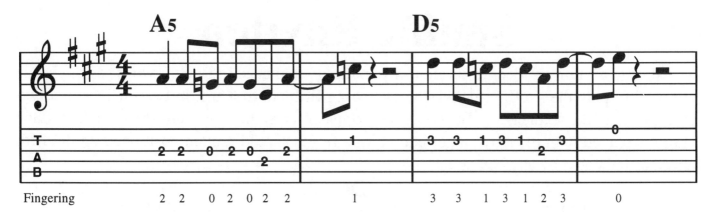

Fingering  2 2   0 2 0 2 2      1       3 3   1 3 1 2 3       0

0 4 3   1 3 1 2 3        3   1 2 2        2   0 2 0 2 0 2          2

# Right Hand Damping

A popular effect to use with the fifth chord is right hand damping. This is achieved by lightly resting the butt of the right hand on the strings near the bridge of the guitar while strumming, producing a slightly muted sound to the chord. Do not press too heavily on the strings as the chord will be completely muted creating a "dead" sound instead.

*Rest butt of hand on strings*

## Example 37

The symbol "D" written above the strumming arrow will indicate when a right hand damp is used. Listen carefully to the recording to hear the desired sound needed for Example 37. An E5 is used.

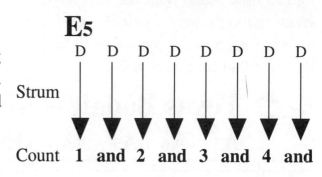

## Example 38

Apply the right hand damp to the following progression.

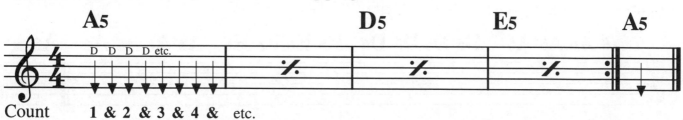

# Lesson 19
## Shuffle Rhythm

The shuffle rhythm or "boogie" is another popular rhythm used in Rock. Two types of chords are used to play the shuffle rhythm, the two string fifth chord learnt in Lesson 18 and a two string form of the sixth chord. The two string forms of the sixth chords are shown below. Each chord is played with the third finger but the first finger should remain positioned on the fifth chord as indicated by an open circle.

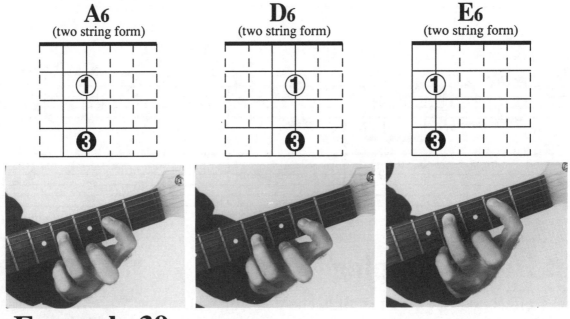

**A6** (two string form)  **D6** (two string form)  **E6** (two string form)

 **Example 39**

Example 39 uses the A5 and A6 chords shown above. To achieve the correct sound for the shuffle rhythm, the first strum of each chord should have a slightly longer time value than the second strum creating the rhythm 1…ah, 2…ah, 3…ah, 4…ah. Listen to the recording to help get the right feel for this rhythm.

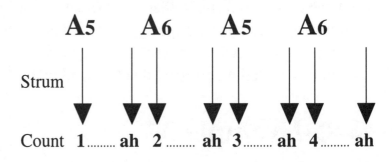

| **A5** | **A6** | **A5** | **A6** |

Strum

Count  1………  ah  2………  ah  3………  ah  4………  ah

 **Texas Boogie – Rhythm**

A5  A6  A5  A6    E5 E6 E5 E6  E5 E6 E5 E6  A5 A6 A5 A6

Count        1……ah 2……ah 3……ah 4……ah  etc.

A5 A6 A5 A6    D5 D6 D5 D6    E5 E6 E5 E6    A5 A6 A5 A6    A5

## Texas Boogie – Lead

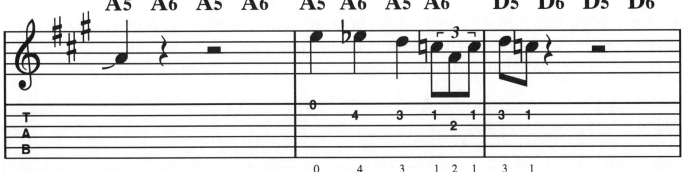

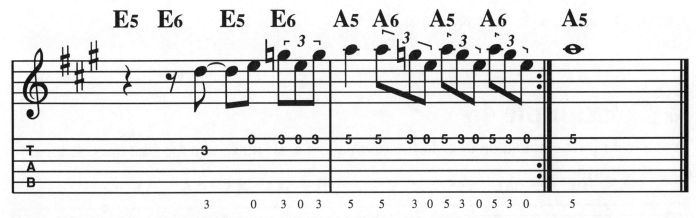

 # Example 40

Example 40 is a popular variation of the shuffle rhythm. The same chords are used but are allocated to different strums within the rhythm.

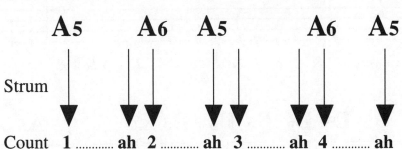

# Example 41

Apply the shuffle rhythm variation from Example 40 to the following chord progression.

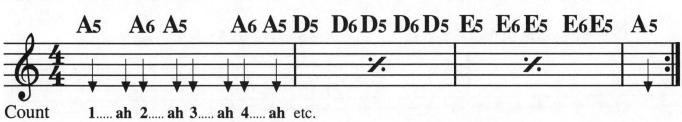

Count    1..... ah 2..... ah 3..... ah 4..... ah etc.

# Lesson 20
## Combining Notes and Chords

It is common practice for Rock guitarists to combine notes and chords together, rather than only play a rhythm part or lead part by itself. The examples in this lesson combine notes and chords using many of the techniques outlined earlier in this book.

### 💿 Example 42

Example 42 combines an A5 chord with a riff on the sixth string. For ease of reading, both the rhythm pattern and the notes are written on the tab lines. Note: the initials N.C. are an abbreviation for "no chord" meaning no chord shape is fingered with the left hand.

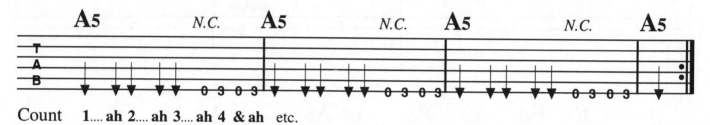

Count      1.... ah 2.... ah 3.... ah 4 & ah   etc.

### 💿 Example 43

Example 43 is a combination of a shuffle rhythm and a riff played on the first three strings.

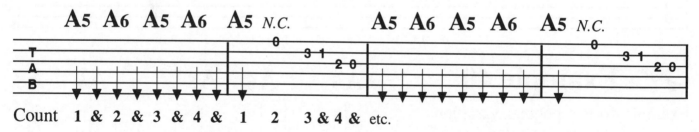

Count   1 & 2 & 3 & 4 &   1   2   3 & 4 &  etc.

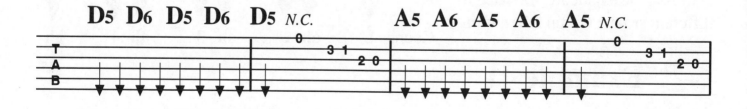

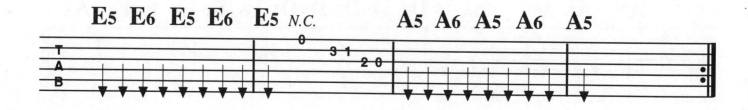

# 💿 Example 44

The rhythm used in Example 44 is a variation of the sixteenth note rhythm, counted 1 and ah, 2 and ah, 3 and ah, 4 and ah. This time part of the chords C and G are fingered with the left hand, while the right hand picks notes on the 5th, 4th and 3rd strings. Chord diagrams have been included to illustrate exactly how both part chords should be fingered.

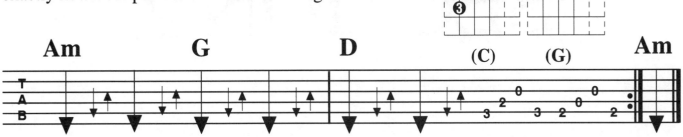

Count 1 & ah 2 & ah 3 & ah 4 & ah 1 & ah 2 & ah 3 e & ah 4 e & ah etc.

# 💿 Example 45

The next example in this lesson demonstrates how a complete chord shape can be fingered with the left hand, while the right hand individually picks each string.

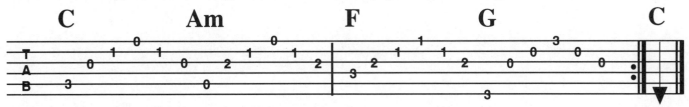

Count 1 & ah 2 & ah 3 & ah 4 & ah etc.

# 💿 Example 46

The final example in this lesson combines a riff played on the bass strings with the E7, A7 and B7 chords.

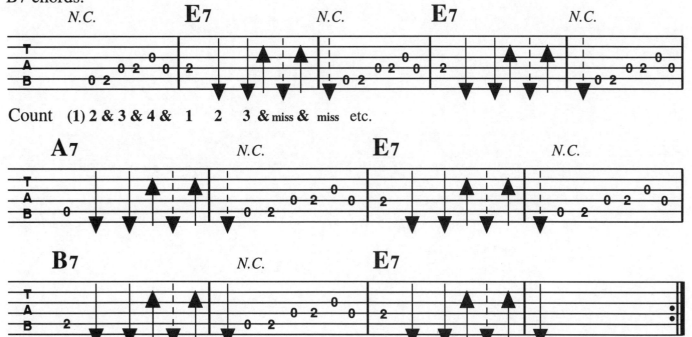

Count (1) 2 & 3 & 4 & 1 2 3 & miss & miss etc.

# SECTION 2

# Appendices

# Appendix I
## Tuning

## Tuning to the Cassette or CD

At the beginning of the accompanying recording, there is a special tuning section. The correct pitch for each string has been recorded several times, giving you the opportunity to compare the pitch of each individual string on your guitar. As each string is sounded on the recording, adjust the pitch of the same string on your guitar by tuning the corresponding tuning peg. To raise the pitch of the string, the string must be tightened. To lower the pitch of the string, the string must be loosened.

## Electronic Guitar Tuner

The easiest and most accurate way to tune a guitar is by means of an electronic guitar tuner. There are several types of electronic guitar tuners but most are relatively inexpensive and simple to operate.

*Electronic Guitar Tuner*

## Tuning the Guitar to Itself

Of none of the above alternatives is possible, try the following procedure.

*Step 1:* Adjust the pitch of the sixth string (E) so it is not too loose or too tight, accepting it is close enough to the note E.

*Step 2:* Adjust the pitch of the fifth string (A) so it is the same pitch as the fifth fret of the sixth string (an A note).

*Step 3:* Adjust the pitch of the fourth string (D) so it is the same pitch as the fifth fret of the fifth string (a D note).

*Step 4:* Adjust the pitch of the third string (G) so it is the same pitch as the fifth fret of the fourth string (a G note).

*Step 5:* Adjust the pitch of the second string (B) so it is the same pitch as the fourth fret of the third string (a B note).

*Step 6:* Adjust the pitch of the first string (E) so it is the same pitch as the fifth fret of the second string (an E note).

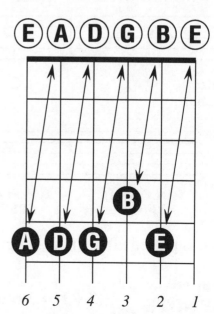

# Appendix II
# The Basics of Music

## The Staff

Music is written on a **Staff**, which consists of 5 parallel lines. **Bar lines** are drawn across the staff, which divide the music into different sections called **Bars** or **Measures**. The end of the music is indicated by a **Double Bar Line**, and two dots placed before a double bar line indicate a **Repeat Sign**. A **Treble Clef** is placed at the beginning of the staff.

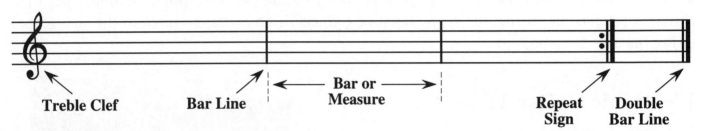

## Notes

Notes can be written on the lines or spaces of the staff and are named as such:

Extra notes can be added by the use of short lines, called **Leger Lines**.

## Note Values

The table below sets out the most common notes used in music and their respective time values (i.e. length of time held). For each note value there is an equivalent rest, which indicates a period of silence.

| | WHOLE NOTE | HALF NOTE | QUARTER NOTE | EIGHTH NOTE | SIXTEENTH NOTE |
|---|---|---|---|---|---|
| Counts (or beats) | 4 | 2 | 1 | $\frac{1}{2}$ | $\frac{1}{4}$ |
| | WHOLE NOTE REST | HALF NOTE REST | QUARTER NOTE REST | EIGHTH NOTE REST | SIXTEENTH NOTE REST |

If a dot is placed after a note it increases the value of the note by half of its original value, e.g.

**Dotted HALF NOTE** $(2 + 1) = 3$ counts

**Dotted QUARTER NOTE** $(1 + \frac{1}{2}) = 1\frac{1}{2}$ counts

# The Tie

A tie is a curved line joining two or more notes of the same pitch. The second note(s) is not played, but its time value is added to that of the first note. Here are two examples:

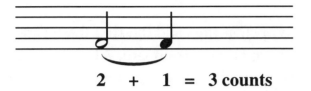

2 + 1 = 3 counts

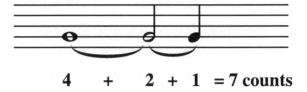

4 + 2 + 1 = 7 counts

# Time Signatures

At the beginning of each piece of music, after the treble clef, is the **time signature.**

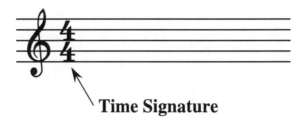

**Time Signature**

The time signature indicates the number of beats per bar (the top number) and the type of note receiving one beat (the bottom number). For example:

**4** – this indicates four beats to the bar.

**4** – this indicates that each beat is worth a quarter note.

Thus in $\frac{4}{4}$ time there must be the equivalent of 4 quarter notes per bar, e.g.

1  2  3  4    1  2  3  4    1  2  3  4    1  2  3  4

$\frac{4}{4}$ is the most common time signature and is sometimes represented by the symbol **C** called **common** time.

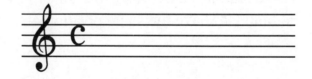

The other time signature used in this book is $\frac{3}{4}$ time, indicating 3 quarter note beats per bar, e.g.

1  2  3    1  2  3    1  2  3    1 + 2  3 +

# Appendix III
## Guitar Music

### Notes in the Open Position

The open position of the guitar contains the notes of the open strings and the first three frets. Outlined below are the position of these notes on the staff and on the fretboard. Also shown is an example of two separate **octaves**, an octave being two notes that have the same letter name and are 8 consecutive notes apart. The example below uses E notes.

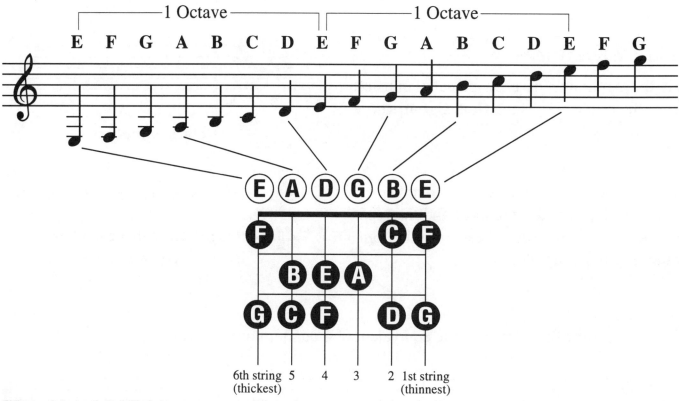

### Sharps and Flats

A **sharp** ( ♯ ) raises the pitch of a note by one semi-tone (1 fret). A **flat** ( ♭ ) lowers the pitch of a note by one semi-tone. In music notation the ♯ and ♭ signs are placed before the note.

The example below also illustrates how the same note can have two different names (i.e. F♯ and G♭ have the same position on the fretboard.

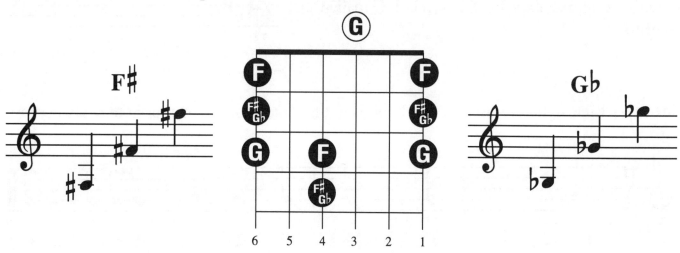

# The Chromatic Scale

With the inclusion of sharps and flats, there are 12 different notes within one octave as shown below. This is commonly known as the **chromatic** scale. Note that there are no sharps or flats between B and C, and E and F.

$$A \quad {A\sharp \atop B\flat} \quad B \quad C \quad {C\sharp \atop D\flat} \quad D \quad {D\sharp \atop E\flat} \quad E \quad F \quad {F\sharp \atop G\flat} \quad G \quad {G\sharp \atop A\flat} \quad A$$

The diagram below displays all the notes in the first position including sharps and flats. The notes on each string are also represented in music.

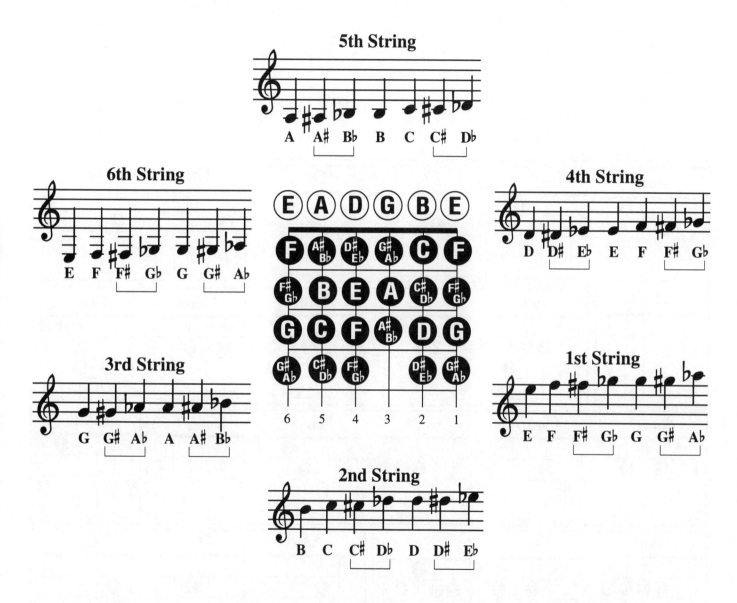

A sharp or flat, when placed before a note, affects the same note if it re-occurs in that bar. It does not, however, affect notes in the next bar. Also used in the following example is a natural sign ( ♮ ) which cancels the effect of a sharp or flat.

# Appendix IV
## Chord Chart

Appendix Four is a summary of all the chords used in this book.

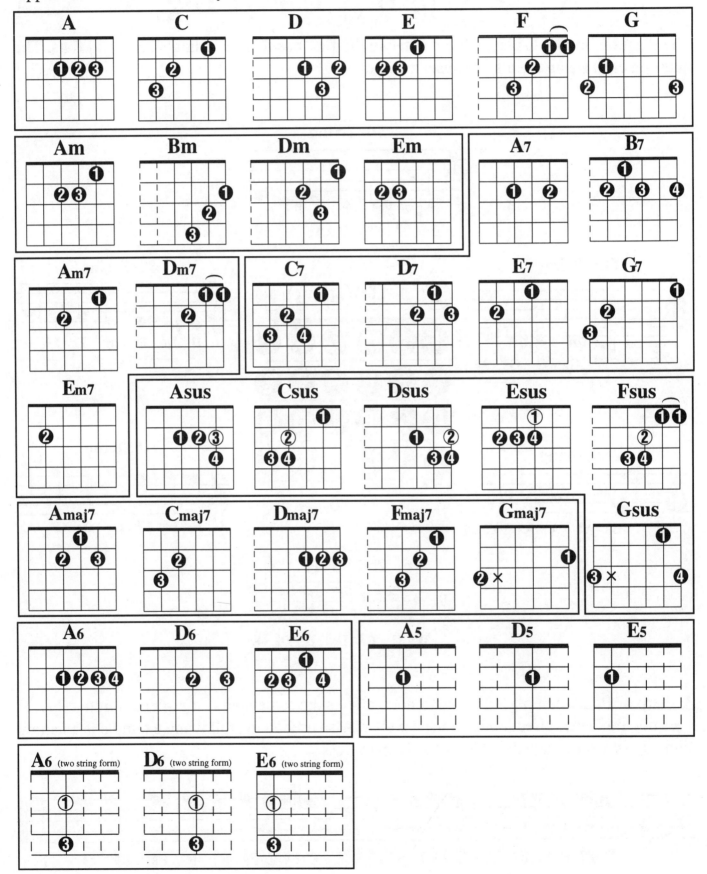